WASH AND DRY

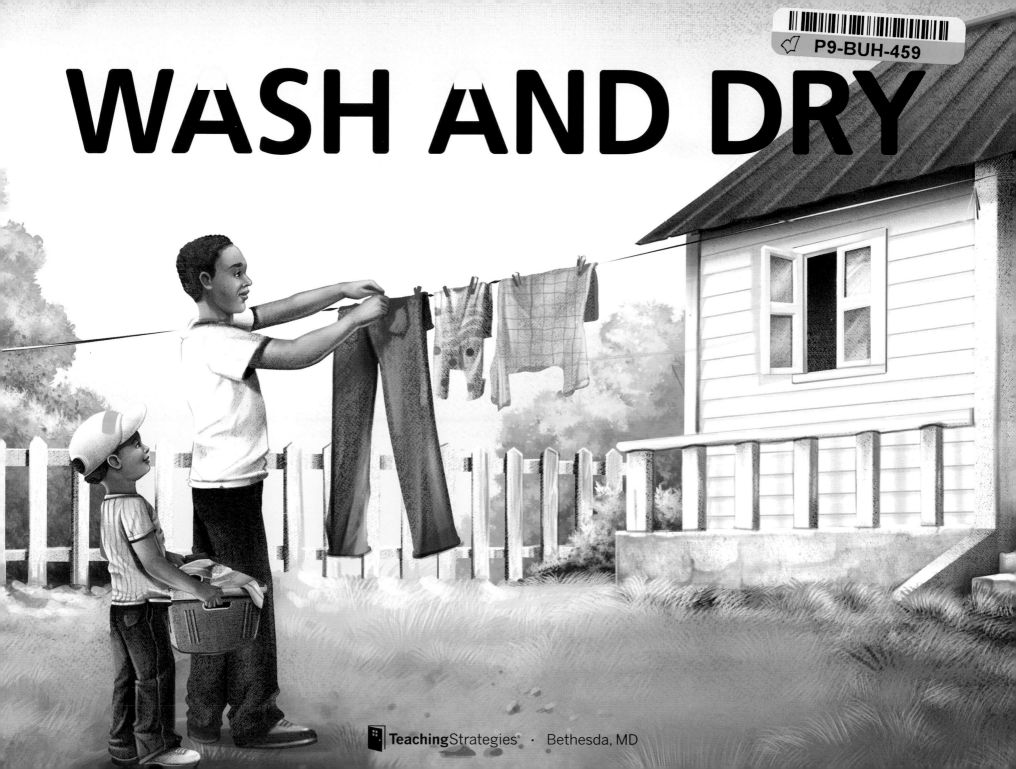

TeachingStrategies® · Bethesda, MD

Teaching Strategies, LLC
Bethesda, MD
www.TeachingStrategies.com

ISBN: 978-1-60617-119-6

Library of Congress Cataloging-in-Publication Data
Holland, Trish.
Wash and dry / written by Trish Holland ; illustrated by Vinay Kumar.
   p. cm.
 ISBN 978-1-60617-119-6
 1. Laundry--Juvenile literature. I. Kumar, Vinay, 1983- II. Title.
 TT985.H65 2010
 648'.1--dc22

                              2009046863

CPSIA tracking label information:
RR Donnelley, Dongguan, China
Date of Production: July 2021
Cohort: Batch 6

Printed and bound in China

14 15 16 17 18 19 20 21 22   27 26 25 24 23 22 21
_____   _____
          Printing   Year Printed

Oh, no! My muddy dog just jumped on me. I'm grimy and slimy from cap to socks. Daddy says I smell like a wet dog. *Peee-uuuw*!

I'll add my dirty clothes to the rest of the dirty laundry. I'm glad Mommy and Daddy will help me wash and dry my clothes. I wouldn't want to have to do *this* job by myself!

Luckily, I still had lots of clean clothes in my dresser. It smells like a bag of lemons in there. I'll be glad when those dirty clothes smell that good.

I carry the stinky basket
over to the washing machine.
I hold my breath as I walk
and try to think about flowers.

It's not working.

I'm glad we have our own washing machine at home. My aunt takes her dirty clothes to the Rub-A-Dub-Tub Laundromat. There are lots of people there, and the machines clink, clank, whistle, and whir as they wash and dry the clothes. My aunt has to use a lot of quarters to wash and dry her clothes.

At our house, Mommy helps me wash my clothes. We put the really dirty clothes in a pile to be washed in the washing machine. It will twist and twirl the dirt right out of the clothes for us.

We put some of the delicate clothes in a pile to wash by hand. We swish and swirl the clothes in the soapy water. There are bubbles in my clothes and bubbles up my nose. *Aaaaah-choooo!*

Before we can put clothes in the washing machine, we have to sort them. We make a pile of the light-colored ones to wash together. If we washed Daddy's dark red shirt with my white underwear, my underwear would turn pink.

We make a pile of dark-colored clothes, too. If we washed my white socks with Mommy's dark blue pants, my socks would be light blue.

We toss a load of dirty clothes in the washer. Then, *clunk*! I shut the door. Mommy lets me pour dry soap powder in the hole at the top of the washer.

Then I add the liquid fabric softener. *Glub, glub, glub!*

Next comes the best part—I get to push the ON button and listen to the machine start to work. *Whoosh*! I watch the sudsy clothes slosh around inside.

I'm looking at my favorite book when I hear *ding*! The washing machine signal tells me that the clothes are ready. They are clean, but still squishy.

Daddy helps me with the next step—drying the clothes. If the sun is shining, we hang them outside on our clothesline. I hand Daddy the clothespins. The clothes will smell like the sun and wind when they are dry.

When it's cloudy, we dry our drippy duds inside the house in the clothes dryer. They flip and fumble and flutter and tumble in the heat. The humming machine is warm. Even our cat likes it when we use the dryer.

Suddenly I hear *buzz*! The clothes are dry, but they are in one big tangle. We all help to fluff and fold the clothes. I like to fold clothes into tidy triangles or silly circles.

Mommy and Daddy fold the clothes into plain rectangles and simple squares. They don't play with the laundry. I think they're missing out on the fun.

Some of the laundry needs
to be hung up on hangers.
Some of it needs to be ironed.
The steam iron hisses while
Daddy irons the wrinkled
shirts. Daddy hisses back.
He doesn't like this part
of laundry.

While Daddy irons, Mommy tells me that a long, long time ago, people washed clothes by pounding them on rocks in a river. Some people still wash their clothes that way. I think I like our way of washing clothes better.

Mommy says that people used to make their own soap. They would boil the ingredients in a big pot over a fire all day long. The soap from each batch would last a long time.

After making all the soap, people scrubbed the dirty clothes on a washboard in a tub. I bet doing laundry took a long, long time!

My great-great-grandmother used a washing machine with a wringer at the top. When she cranked the handle, the wringer squished most of the water out of the clothes.

22

She'd hang her clothes on a clothesline, too. When they were dry, she used a giant ironing machine called a mangle. She'd crank that handle, and the clothes would go in all wrinkled and come out smooth.

I'm glad we don't have to work so hard at washing clothes. I can put on my favorite outfit and not smell like a wet dog.

Oh, noooooooooo! Here we go again!